CW00536676

A LITTLE BOOK OF

Welsh
Sayings

Compiled by Meic Stephens

Appletree Press

First published in 1998 by
Appletree Press Ltd
The Old Potato Station
14 Howard Street South
Belfast BT7 1AP
Tel: +44 (0) 28 90 243074
Fax: +44 (0) 28 90 246756
Web site: www.appletree.ie
Email: reception@appletree.ie

A Little Book of Welsh Sayings

A catalogue record for this book
is available from the British Library.

ISBN 0 86281 703 X

9 8 7 6 5 4 3

Note: Text marked with an asterisk
has been translated from Welsh.

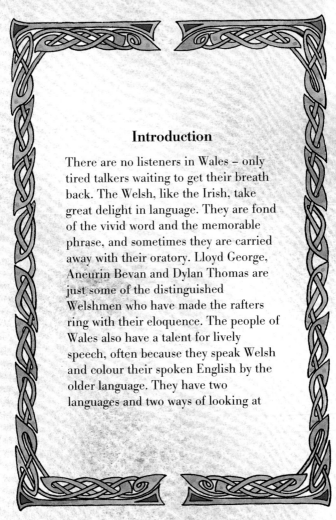

Introduction

There are no listeners in Wales – only tired talkers waiting to get their breath back. The Welsh, like the Irish, take great delight in language. They are fond of the vivid word and the memorable phrase, and sometimes they are carried away with their oratory. Lloyd George, Aneurin Bevan and Dylan Thomas are just some of the distinguished Welshmen who have made the rafters ring with their eloquence. The people of Wales also have a talent for lively speech, often because they speak Welsh and colour their spoken English by the older language. They have two languages and two ways of looking at

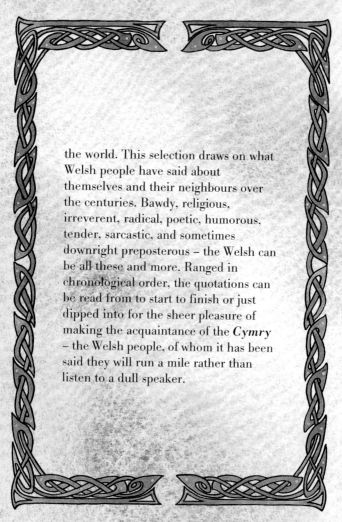

the world. This selection draws on what Welsh people have said about themselves and their neighbours over the centuries. Bawdy, religious, irreverent, radical, poetic, humorous, tender, sarcastic, and sometimes downright preposterous – the Welsh can be all these and more. Ranged in chronological order, the quotations can be read from to start to finish or just dipped into for the sheer pleasure of making the acquaintance of the *Cymry* – the Welsh people, of whom it has been said they will run a mile rather than listen to a dull speaker.

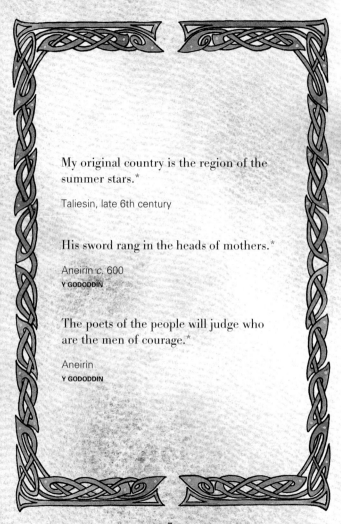

My original country is the region of the summer stars.*

Taliesin, late 6th century

His sword rang in the heads of mothers.*

Aneirin c. 600
Y GODODDIN

The poets of the people will judge who are the men of courage.*

Aneirin
Y GODODDIN

The four chief things I hated now come
all at once:
Coughing and old age, sickness and
sorrow.*

Anonymous, 9th century
CANU LLYWARCH HEN

I am old, bent in three, I am fickle,
    reckless,
I'm a fool and uncouth,
They who once loved me love me no
    more.*

Anonymous, 9th century
CANU LLYWARCH HEN

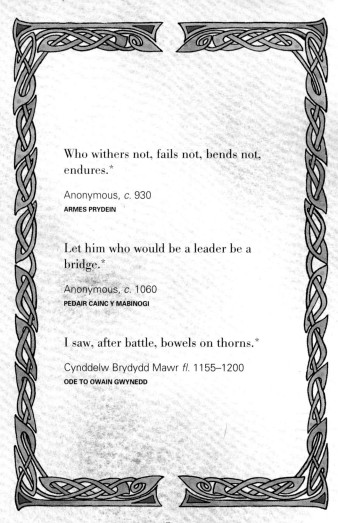

Who withers not, fails not, bends not, endures.*

Anonymous, c. 930
ARMES PRYDEIN

Let him who would be a leader be a bridge.*

Anonymous, c. 1060
PEDAIR CAINC Y MABINOGI

I saw, after battle, bowels on thorns.*

Cynddelw Brydydd Mawr *fl.* 1155–1200
ODE TO OWAIN GWYNEDD

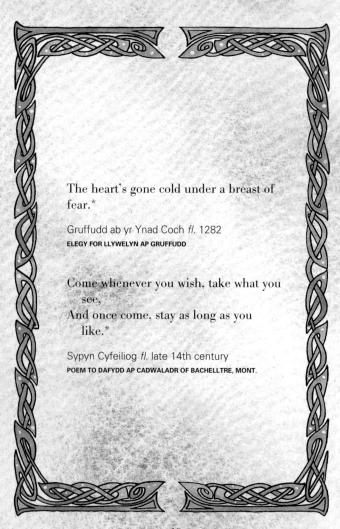

The heart's gone cold under a breast of
fear.*

Gruffudd ab yr Ynad Coch *fl.* 1282
ELEGY FOR LLYWELYN AP GRUFFUDD

Come whenever you wish, take what you
    see,
And once come, stay as long as you
    like.*

Sypyn Cyfeiliog *fl.* late 14th century
POEM TO DAFYDD AP CADWALADR OF BACHELLTRE, MONT.

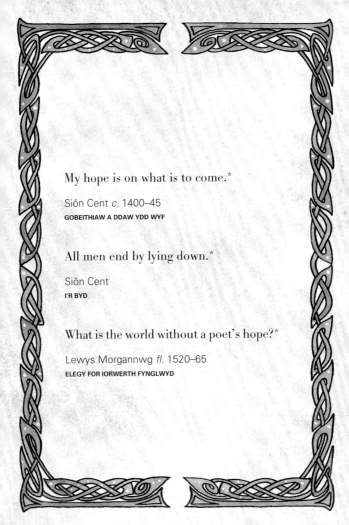

My hope is on what is to come.*

Siôn Cent c. 1400–45
GOBEITHIAW A DDAW YDD WYF

All men end by lying down.*

Siôn Cent
I'R BYD

What is the world without a poet's hope?*

Lewys Morgannwg fl. 1520–65
ELEGY FOR IORWERTH FYNGLWYD

11

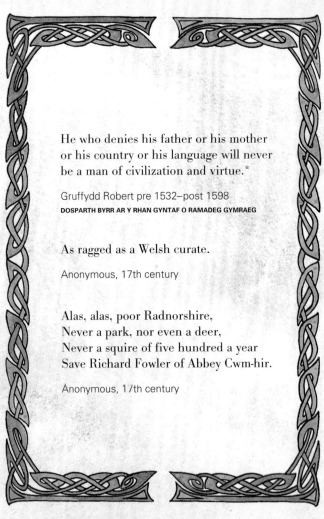

He who denies his father or his mother
or his country or his language will never
be a man of civilization and virtue.*

Gruffydd Robert pre 1532–post 1598
DOSPARTH BYRR AR Y RHAN GYNTAF O RAMADEG GYMRAEG

As ragged as a Welsh curate.

Anonymous, 17th century

Alas, alas, poor Radnorshire,
Never a park, nor even a deer,
Never a squire of five hundred a year
Save Richard Fowler of Abbey Cwm-hir.

Anonymous, 17th century

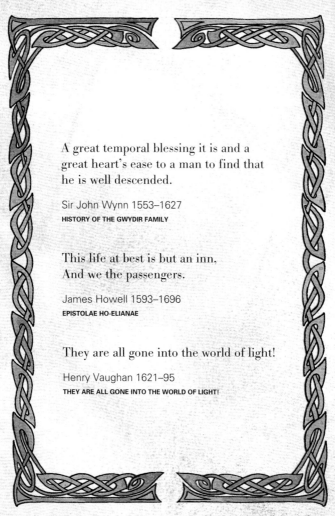

A great temporal blessing it is and a great heart's ease to a man to find that he is well descended.

Sir John Wynn 1553–1627
HISTORY OF THE GWYDIR FAMILY

This life at best is but an inn,
And we the passengers.

James Howell 1593–1696
EPISTOLAE HO-ELIANAE

They are all gone into the world of light!

Henry Vaughan 1621–95
THEY ARE ALL GONE INTO THE WORLD OF LIGHT!

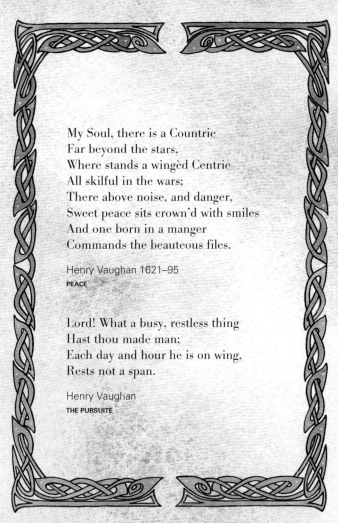

My Soul, there is a Countrie
Far beyond the stars,
Where stands a wingèd Centrie
All skilful in the wars;
There above noise, and danger,
Sweet peace sits crown'd with smiles
And one born in a manger
Commands the beauteous files.

Henry Vaughan 1621–95
PEACE

Lord! What a busy, restless thing
Hast thou made man;
Each day and hour he is on wing,
Rests not a span.

Henry Vaughan
THE PURSUITE

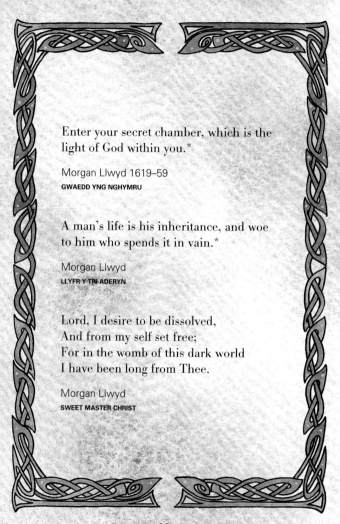

Enter your secret chamber, which is the
light of God within you.*

Morgan Llwyd 1619–59
GWAEDD YNG NGHYMRU

A man's life is his inheritance, and woe
to him who spends it in vain.*

Morgan Llwyd
LLYFR Y TRI ADERYN

Lord, I desire to be dissolved,
And from my self set free;
For in the womb of this dark world
I have been long from Thee.

Morgan Llwyd
SWEET MASTER CHRIST

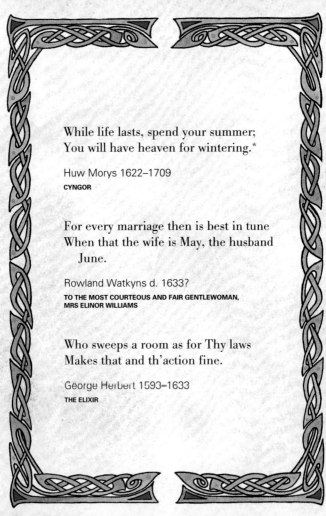

While life lasts, spend your summer;
You will have heaven for wintering.*

Huw Morys 1622–1709
CYNGOR

For every marriage then is best in tune
When that the wife is May, the husband
   June.

Rowland Watkyns d. 1633?
**TO THE MOST COURTEOUS AND FAIR GENTLEWOMAN,
MRS ELINOR WILLIAMS**

Who sweeps a room as for Thy laws
Makes that and th'action fine.

George Herbert 1593–1633
THE ELIXIR

Teach me, my God and King,
In all things Thee to see,
And what I do in any thing
To do it as for Thee.

George Herbert
THE ELIXIR

Throw away thy rod,
Throw away thy wrath,
O my God, take the gentle path.

George Herbert
THE TEMPLE

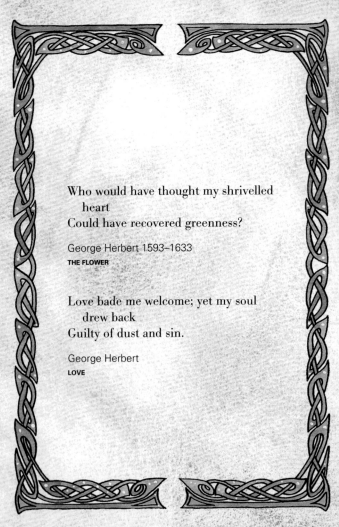

Who would have thought my shrivelled
    heart
Could have recovered greenness?

George Herbert 1593–1633
THE FLOWER

Love bade me welcome; yet my soul
    drew back
Guilty of dust and sin.

George Herbert
LOVE

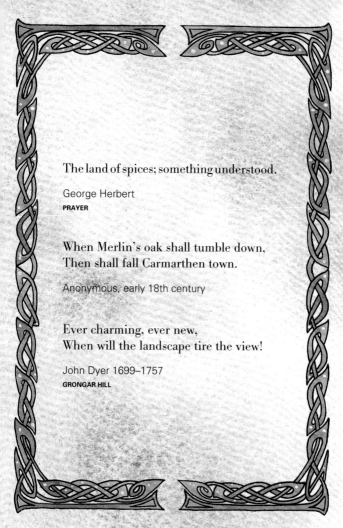

The land of spices; something understood.

George Herbert
PRAYER

When Merlin's oak shall tumble down,
Then shall fall Carmarthen town.

Anonymous, early 18th century

Ever charming, ever new,
When will the landscape tire the view!

John Dyer 1699–1757
GRONGAR HILL

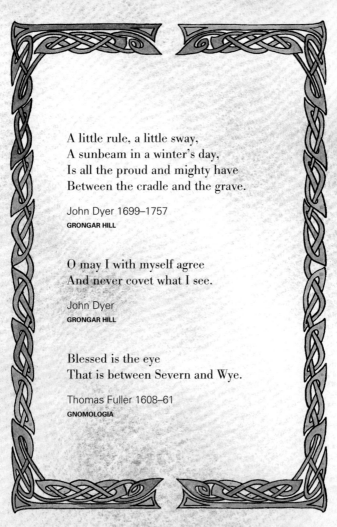

A little rule, a little sway,
A sunbeam in a winter's day,
Is all the proud and mighty have
Between the cradle and the grave.

John Dyer 1699–1757
GRONGAR HILL

O may I with myself agree
And never covet what I see.

John Dyer
GRONGAR HILL

Blessed is the eye
That is between Severn and Wye.

Thomas Fuller 1608–61
GNOMOLOGIA

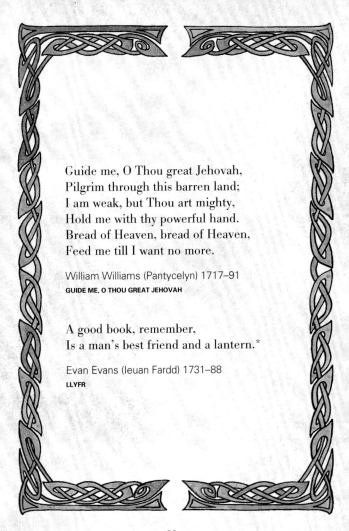

Guide me, O Thou great Jehovah,
Pilgrim through this barren land;
I am weak, but Thou art mighty,
Hold me with thy powerful hand.
Bread of Heaven, bread of Heaven,
Feed me till I want no more.

William Williams (Pantycelyn) 1717–91
GUIDE ME, O THOU GREAT JEHOVAH

A good book, remember,
Is a man's best friend and a lantern.*

Evan Evans (Ieuan Fardd) 1731–88
LLYFR

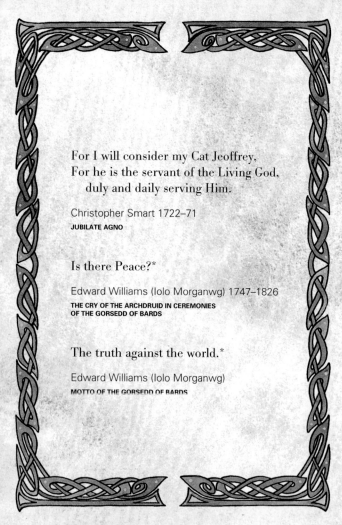

For I will consider my Cat Jeoffrey,
For he is the servant of the Living God,
   duly and daily serving Him.

Christopher Smart 1722–71
JUBILATE AGNO

Is there Peace?*

Edward Williams (Iolo Morganwg) 1747–1826
**THE CRY OF THE ARCHDRUID IN CEREMONIES
OF THE GORSEDD OF BARDS**

The truth against the world.*

Edward Williams (Iolo Morganwg)
MOTTO OF THE GORSEDD OF BARDS

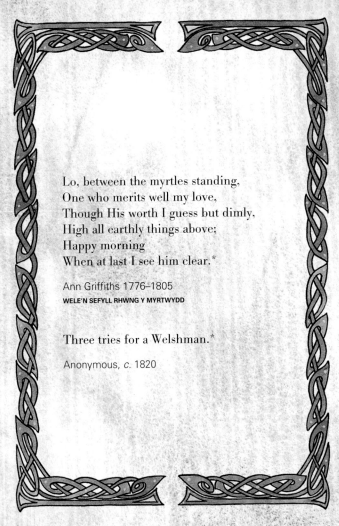

Lo, between the myrtles standing,
One who merits well my love,
Though His worth I guess but dimly,
High all earthly things above;
Happy morning
When at last I see him clear.*

Ann Griffiths 1776–1805
WELE'N SEFYLL RHWNG Y MYRTWYDD

Three tries for a Welshman.*

Anonymous, *c.* 1820

23

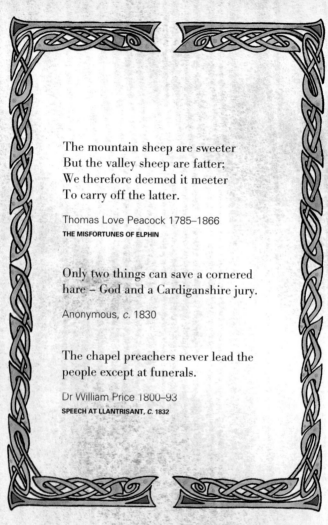

The mountain sheep are sweeter
But the valley sheep are fatter;
We therefore deemed it meeter
To carry off the latter.

Thomas Love Peacock 1785–1866
THE MISFORTUNES OF ELPHIN

Only two things can save a cornered
hare – God and a Cardiganshire jury.

Anonymous, *c.* 1830

The chapel preachers never lead the
people except at funerals.

Dr William Price 1800–93
SPEECH AT LLANTRISANT, *C.* **1832**

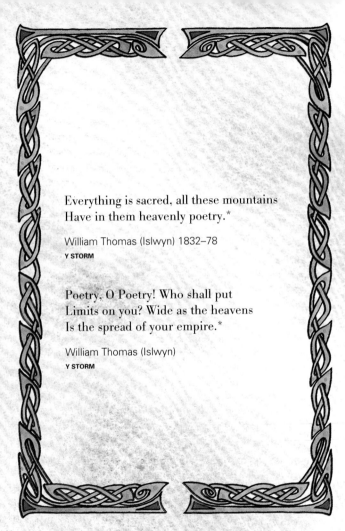

Everything is sacred, all these mountains
Have in them heavenly poetry.*

William Thomas (Islwyn) 1832–78
Y STORM

Poetry, O Poetry! Who shall put
Limits on you? Wide as the heavens
Is the spread of your empire.*

William Thomas (Islwyn)
Y STORM

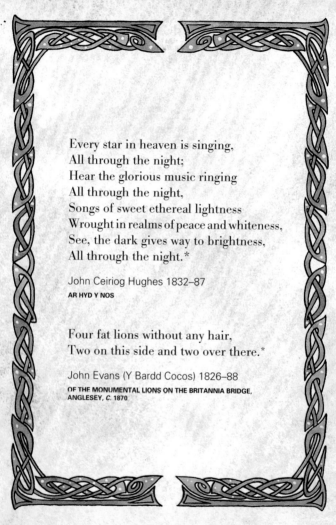

Every star in heaven is singing,
All through the night;
Hear the glorious music ringing
All through the night,
Songs of sweet ethereal lightness
Wrought in realms of peace and whiteness,
See, the dark gives way to brightness,
All through the night.*

John Ceiriog Hughes 1832–87
AR HYD Y NOS

Four fat lions without any hair,
Two on this side and two over there.*

John Evans (Y Bardd Cocos) 1826–88
OF THE MONUMENTAL LIONS ON THE BRITANNIA BRIDGE,
ANGLESEY, C. 1870

Dr Livingstone, I presume?

Henry Morton Stanley 1841–1904
ON FINDING THE EXPLORER AT UJIJI, 1871

God forgive me.

Anonymous,
**INSCRIPTION ON GRAVESTONE OF THE
IRONMASTER ROBERT THOMPSON CRAWSHAY, 1879**

It came to pass in days of yore,
The Devil chanced upon Llandore;
Quoth he, By all this fume and stink,
I can't be far from home, I think.

Anonymous, *c.* 1890

The life of one Welsh miner is of greater commercial and moral value than the whole royal crowd put together.

Keir Hardie 1856–1915

IN LABOUR LEADER, 1894

Yes, Home Rule for Hell! I like every man to speak up for his own country.

David Lloyd George 1863–1945

IN RESPONSE TO HECKLER WHO HAD SHOUTED "'OME RULE FOR 'ELL!", 1894

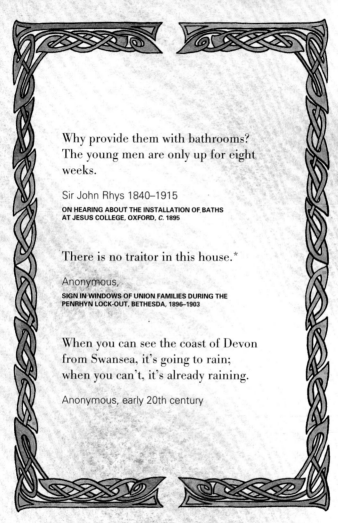

Why provide them with bathrooms?
The young men are only up for eight
weeks.

Sir John Rhys 1840–1915

ON HEARING ABOUT THE INSTALLATION OF BATHS
AT JESUS COLLEGE, OXFORD, C. 1895

There is no traitor in this house.*

Anonymous,

SIGN IN WINDOWS OF UNION FAMILIES DURING THE
PENRHYN LOCK-OUT, BETHESDA, 1896–1903

When you can see the coast of Devon
from Swansea, it's going to rain;
when you can't, it's already raining.

Anonymous, early 20th century

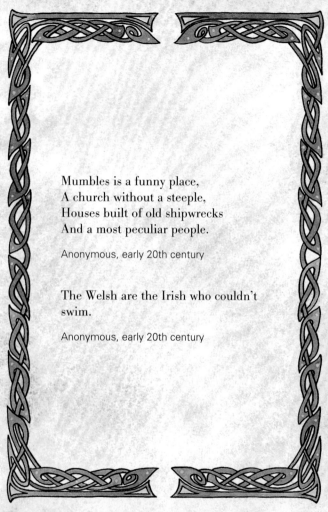

Mumbles is a funny place,
A church without a steeple,
Houses built of old shipwrecks
And a most peculiar people.

Anonymous, early 20th century

The Welsh are the Irish who couldn't
swim.

Anonymous, early 20th century

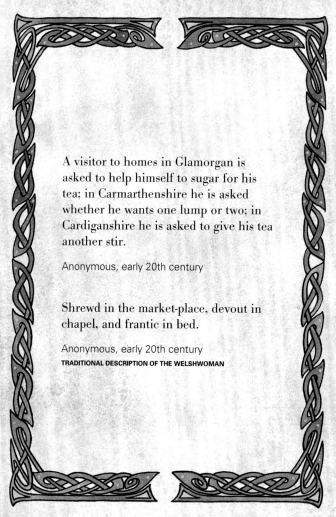

A visitor to homes in Glamorgan is asked to help himself to sugar for his tea; in Carmarthenshire he is asked whether he wants one lump or two; in Cardiganshire he is asked to give his tea another stir.

Anonymous, early 20th century

Shrewd in the market-place, devout in chapel, and frantic in bed.

Anonymous, early 20th century

TRADITIONAL DESCRIPTION OF THE WELSHWOMAN

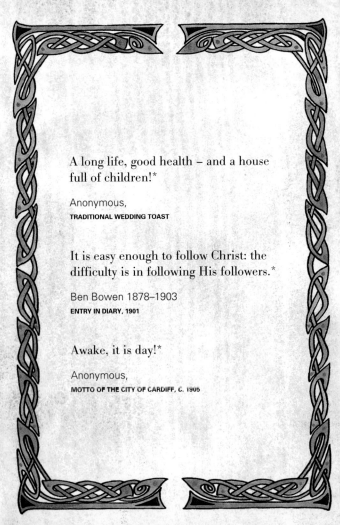

A long life, good health – and a house full of children!*

Anonymous,
TRADITIONAL WEDDING TOAST

It is easy enough to follow Christ: the difficulty is in following His followers.*

Ben Bowen 1878–1903
ENTRY IN DIARY, 1901

Awake, it is day!*

Anonymous,
MOTTO OF THE CITY OF CARDIFF, c. 1905

Girls scream,
Boys shout;
Dogs bark,
School's out.

W.H. Davies 1871–1940
SCHOOL'S OUT

Five hundred men, ordinary men,
chosen accidentally from among the
unemployed.

David Lloyd George 1863–1945
OF THE HOUSE OF LORDS IN SPEECH, 1909

It was the rainbow gave thee birth,
And left thee all her lovely hues.

W.H. Davies
THE KINGFISHER

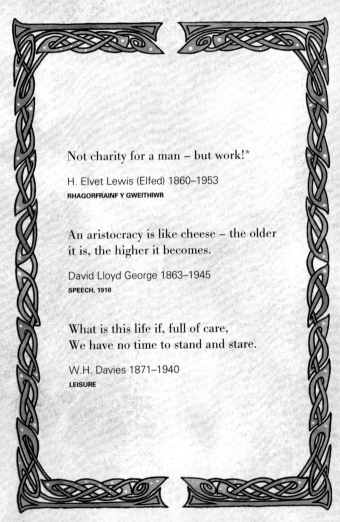

Not charity for a man – but work!*

H. Elvet Lewis (Elfed) 1860–1953
RHAGORFRAINF Y GWEITHIWR

An aristocracy is like cheese – the older
it is, the higher it becomes.

David Lloyd George 1863–1945
SPEECH, 1910

What is this life if, full of care,
We have no time to stand and stare.

W.H. Davies 1871–1940
LEISURE

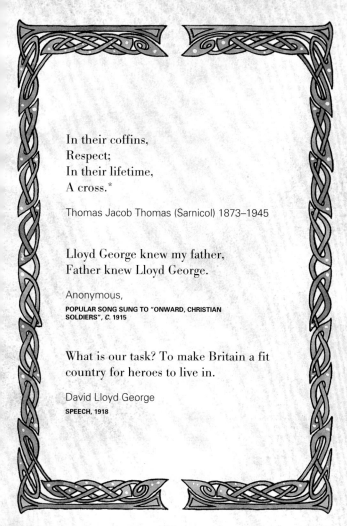

In their coffins,
Respect;
In their lifetime,
A cross.*

Thomas Jacob Thomas (Sarnicol) 1873–1945

Lloyd George knew my father,
Father knew Lloyd George.

Anonymous,
POPULAR SONG SUNG TO "ONWARD, CHRISTIAN SOLDIERS", C. 1915

What is our task? To make Britain a fit country for heroes to live in.

David Lloyd George
SPEECH, 1918

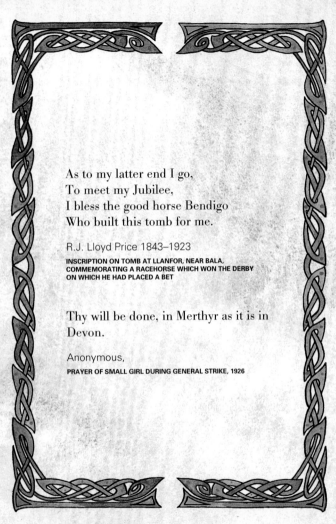

As to my latter end I go,
To meet my Jubilee,
I bless the good horse Bendigo
Who built this tomb for me.

R.J. Lloyd Price 1843–1923

INSCRIPTION ON TOMB AT LLANFOR, NEAR BALA,
COMMEMORATING A RACEHORSE WHICH WON THE DERBY
ON WHICH HE HAD PLACED A BET

Thy will be done, in Merthyr as it is in
Devon.

Anonymous,

PRAYER OF SMALL GIRL DURING GENERAL STRIKE, 1926

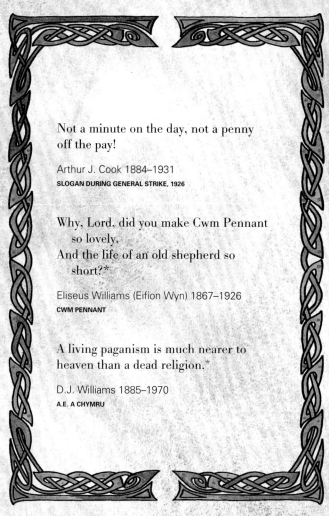

Not a minute on the day, not a penny
off the pay!

Arthur J. Cook 1884–1931
SLOGAN DURING GENERAL STRIKE, 1926

Why, Lord, did you make Cwm Pennant
   so lovely,
And the life of an old shepherd so
   short?*

Eliseus Williams (Eifion Wyn) 1867–1926
CWM PENNANT

A living paganism is much nearer to
heaven than a dead religion.*

D.J. Williams 1885–1970
A.E. A CHYMRU

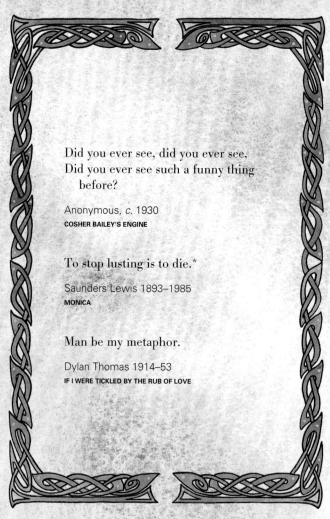

Did you ever see, did you ever see.
Did you ever see such a funny thing
    before?

Anonymous, *c.* 1930
COSHER BAILEY'S ENGINE

To stop lusting is to die.*

Saunders Lewis 1893–1985
MONICA

Man be my metaphor.

Dylan Thomas 1914–53
IF I WERE TICKLED BY THE RUB OF LOVE

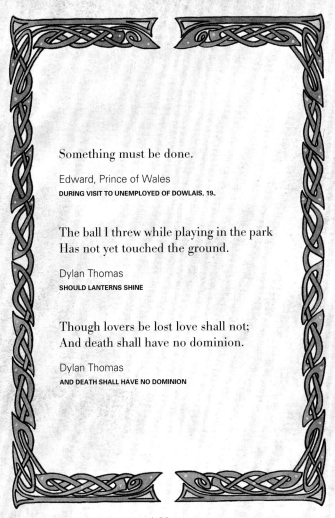

Something must be done.

Edward, Prince of Wales
DURING VISIT TO UNEMPLOYED OF DOWLAIS, 19.

The ball I threw while playing in the park
Has not yet touched the ground.

Dylan Thomas
SHOULD LANTERNS SHINE

Though lovers be lost love shall not;
And death shall have no dominion.

Dylan Thomas
AND DEATH SHALL HAVE NO DOMINION

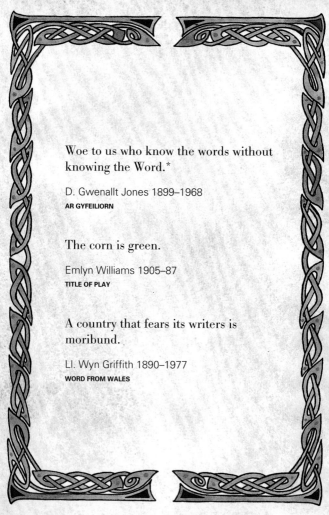

Woe to us who know the words without knowing the Word.*

D. Gwenallt Jones 1899–1968
AR GYFEILIORN

The corn is green.

Emlyn Williams 1905–87
TITLE OF PLAY

A country that fears its writers is moribund.

Ll. Wyn Griffith 1890–1977
WORD FROM WALES

Blue necklace left
On a charred chair
Tells that beauty
Was startled there.

Alun Lewis 1915–44
RAIDERS' DAWN

If I should go away,
Beloved, do not say
"He has forgotten me."
For you abide,
A singing rib within my dreaming side;
You always stay.

Alun Lewis
POST-SCRIPT: FOR GWENNO

Keep your bloody chips!*

T. Rowland Hughes 1903–49
WILLIAM JONES

Here I stand, a middle-aged master.
When my heart went to stone and my
    world to disaster
I repaired my glasses with surgical
    plaster.

Glyn Jones 1905–95
THE DREAM OF JAKE HOPKINS

So we must say Goodbye, my darling.
And go, as lovers go, for ever;
Tonight remains, to pack and fix on labels
And make an end of lying down together.

Alun Lewis 1915–44
GOODBYE

It was my thirtieth year to heaven.

Dylan Thomas 1914–53
POEM IN OCTOBER

After the first death there is no other.

Dylan Thomas 1914–53
A REFUSAL TO MOURN THE DEATH, BY FIRE, OF A CHILD IN LONDON

43

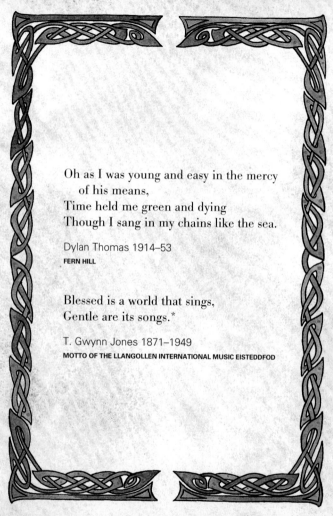

Oh as I was young and easy in the mercy
    of his means,
Time held me green and dying
Though I sang in my chains like the sea.

Dylan Thomas 1914–53
FERN HILL

Blessed is a world that sings,
Gentle are its songs.*

T. Gwynn Jones 1871–1949
MOTTO OF THE LLANGOLLEN INTERNATIONAL MUSIC EISTEDDFOD

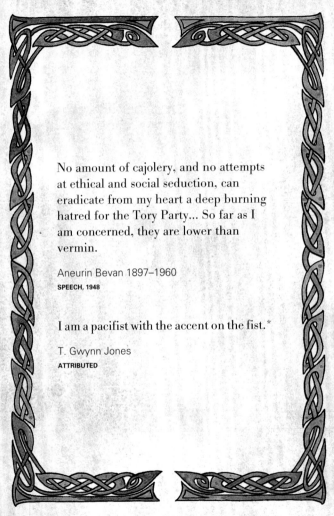

No amount of cajolery, and no attempts at ethical and social seduction, can eradicate from my heart a deep burning hatred for the Tory Party... So far as I am concerned, they are lower than vermin.

Aneurin Bevan 1897–1960
SPEECH, 1948

I am a pacifist with the accent on the fist.*

T. Gwynn Jones
ATTRIBUTED

Swansea man weds Swansea woman in Swansea.

Anonymous,
HEADLINE IN THE SOUTH WALES EVENING POST 1952

Do not go gentle into that good night.

Dylan Thomas 1914–53
DO NOT GO GENTLE INTO THAT GOOD NIGHT

Death does not die. This is woe.*

R. Williams Parry 1884–1956
YMSON YNGHYLCH AMSER

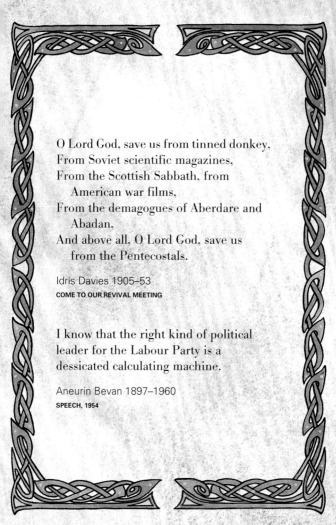

O Lord God, save us from tinned donkey,
From Soviet scientific magazines,
From the Scottish Sabbath, from
   American war films,
From the demagogues of Aberdare and
   Abadan,
And above all, O Lord God, save us
   from the Pentecostals.

Idris Davies 1905–53
COME TO OUR REVIVAL MEETING

I know that the right kind of political
leader for the Labour Party is a
dessicated calculating machine.

Aneurin Bevan 1897–1960
SPEECH, 1954

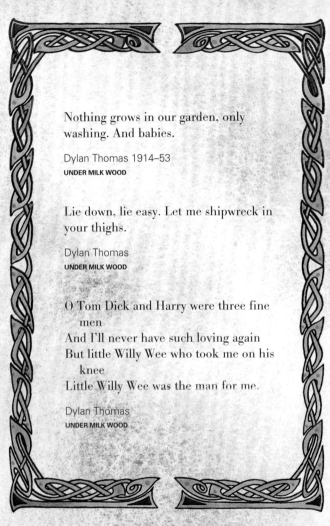

Nothing grows in our garden, only washing. And babies.

Dylan Thomas 1914–53
UNDER MILK WOOD

Lie down, lie easy. Let me shipwreck in your thighs.

Dylan Thomas
UNDER MILK WOOD

O Tom Dick and Harry were three fine
   men
And I'll never have such loving again
But little Willy Wee who took me on his
   knee
Little Willy Wee was the man for me.

Dylan Thomas
UNDER MILK WOOD

I love you until Death do us part and then we shall be together for ever and ever.

Dylan Thomas
UNDER MILK WOOD

Men are brutes on the quiet.

Dylan Thomas
UNDER MILK WOOD

Oh, isn't life a terrible thing, thank God?

Dylan Thomas
UNDER MILK WOOD

And before you let the sun in, mind it wipes its shoes.

Dylan Thomas
UNDER MILK WOOD

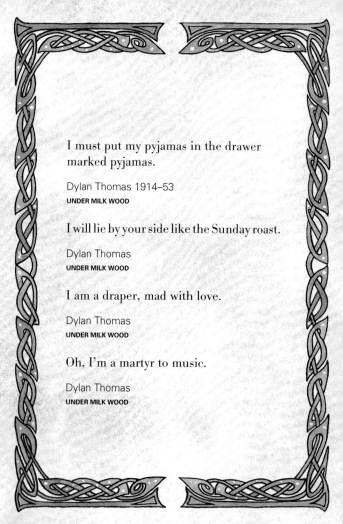

I must put my pyjamas in the drawer
marked pyjamas.

Dylan Thomas 1914–53
UNDER MILK WOOD

I will lie by your side like the Sunday roast.

Dylan Thomas
UNDER MILK WOOD

I am a draper, mad with love.

Dylan Thomas
UNDER MILK WOOD

Oh, I'm a martyr to music.

Dylan Thomas
UNDER MILK WOOD

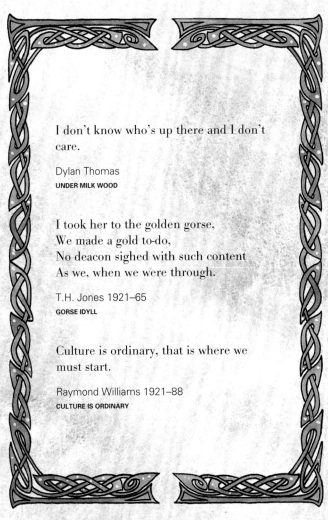

I don't know who's up there and I don't care.

Dylan Thomas
UNDER MILK WOOD

I took her to the golden gorse,
We made a gold to-do,
No deacon sighed with such content
As we, when we were through.

T.H. Jones 1921–65
GORSE IDYLL

Culture is ordinary, that is where we must start.

Raymond Williams 1921–88
CULTURE IS ORDINARY

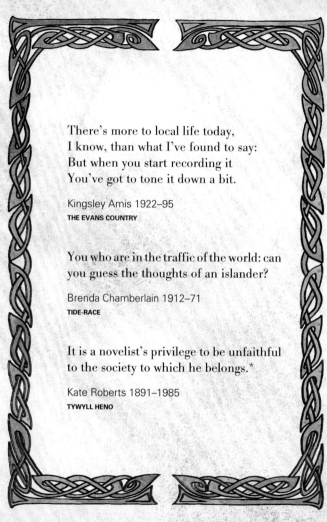

There's more to local life today,
I know, than what I've found to say:
But when you start recording it
You've got to tone it down a bit.

Kingsley Amis 1922–95
THE EVANS COUNTRY

You who are in the traffic of the world: can
you guess the thoughts of an islander?

Brenda Chamberlain 1912–71
TIDE-RACE

It is a novelist's privilege to be unfaithful
to the society to which he belongs.*

Kate Roberts 1891–1985
TYWYLL HENO

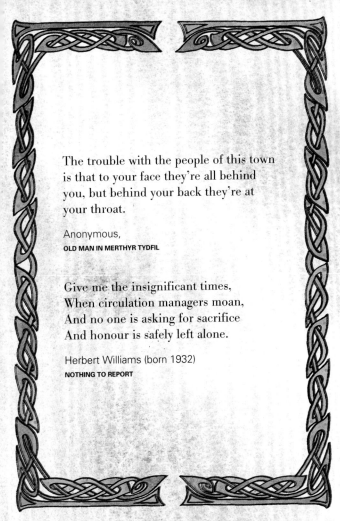

The trouble with the people of this town
is that to your face they're all behind
you, but behind your back they're at
your throat.

Anonymous,
OLD MAN IN MERTHYR TYDFIL

Give me the insignificant times,
When circulation managers moan,
And no one is asking for sacrifice
And honour is safely left alone.

Herbert Williams (born 1932)
NOTHING TO REPORT

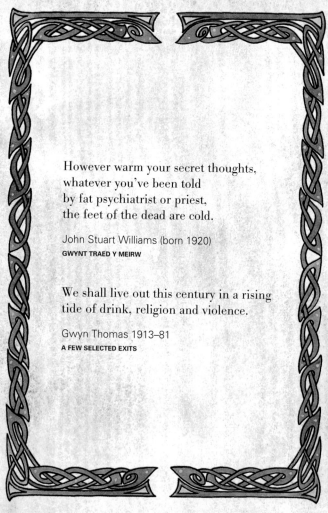

However warm your secret thoughts,
whatever you've been told
by fat psychiatrist or priest,
the feet of the dead are cold.

John Stuart Williams (born 1920)
GWYNT TRAED Y MEIRW

We shall live out this century in a rising
tide of drink, religion and violence.

Gwyn Thomas 1913–81
A FEW SELECTED EXITS

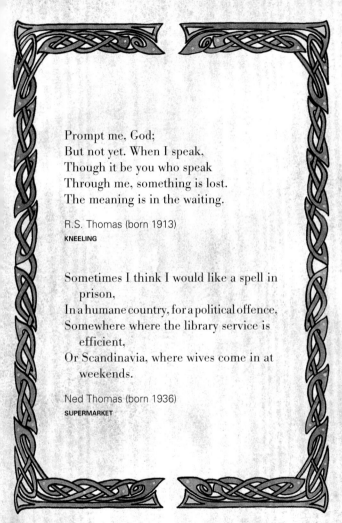

Prompt me, God;
But not yet. When I speak,
Though it be you who speak
Through me, something is lost.
The meaning is in the waiting.

R.S. Thomas (born 1913)
KNEELING

Sometimes I think I would like a spell in
    prison,
In a humane country, for a political offence,
Somewhere where the library service is
    efficient,
Or Scandinavia, where wives come in at
    weekends.

Ned Thomas (born 1936)
SUPERMARKET

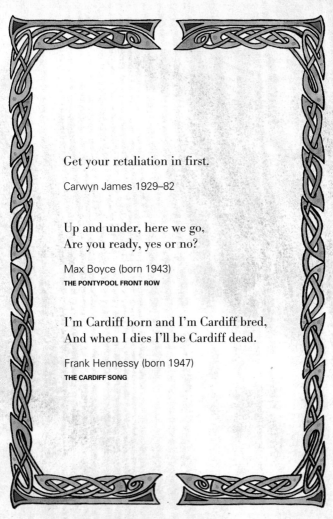

Get your retaliation in first.

Carwyn James 1929–82

Up and under, here we go,
Are you ready, yes or no?

Max Boyce (born 1943)
THE PONTYPOOL FRONT ROW

I'm Cardiff born and I'm Cardiff bred,
And when I dies I'll be Cardiff dead.

Frank Hennessy (born 1947)
THE CARDIFF SONG

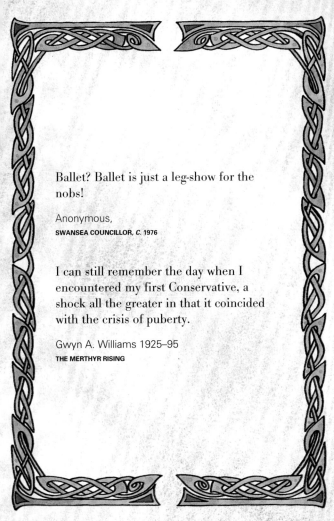

Ballet? Ballet is just a leg-show for the nobs!

Anonymous,
SWANSEA COUNCILLOR, *C.* **1976**

I can still remember the day when I encountered my first Conservative, a shock all the greater in that it coincided with the crisis of puberty.

Gwyn A. Williams 1925–95
THE MERTHYR RISING

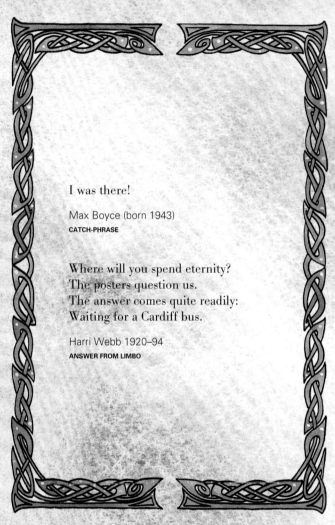

I was there!

Max Boyce (born 1943)
CATCH-PHRASE

Where will you spend eternity?
The posters question us.
The answer comes quite readily:
Waiting for a Cardiff bus.

Harri Webb 1920–94
ANSWER FROM LIMBO